12930

**920
MC**   **McReynolds, Ginny.**

       Women in power.

                                    $9.98

DATE DUE	BORROWER'S NAME	ROOM NO.

12930

920   McReynolds, Ginny.
MC
       Women in power.

Women in Power

Cover by Jackie Denison

Illustrations by Jane Palecek

Copyright © 1979, Raintree Publishers Limited

Library of Congress Number: 79-13301

1 2 3 4 5 6 7 8 9 0 83 82 81 80 79

Printed and bound in the United States of America.

Library of Congress Cataloging in Publication Data
McReynolds, Ginny.
    Women in power.
    Bibliography: p. 48.
    SUMMARY: Brief descriptions of the lives, accom-
plishements, and goals of various women prominent in the
field of politics. Includes Ella Grasso, Barbara Jordan,
Golda Meir, and Jeanette Rankin.
    1. Women in politics—Biography—Juvenile literature.
[1. Women in politics. 2. Politics, Practical—
Biography] I. Palecek, Jane. II. Title.
HQ1390.M32   329   [920]   79-13301
ISBN 0-8172-1376-7 lib. bdg.

WOMEN IN POWER

Ginny McReynolds

RAINTREE PUBLISHERS
Milwaukee • Toronto • Melbourne • London

CONTENTS

INTRODUCTION

Women's involvement in U.S. politics began in the early 1800s in Kentucky, where women were allowed to vote in school elections. By 1890, it was acceptable in nineteen states for women to be involved in school politics as voters.

In the early 1900s, many states in the West and Midwest granted general voting rights to women. In these pioneer states, women worked side by side with men, who saw them as equals. Women's voting rights in the East came later.

In 1920, the Nineteenth Amendment to the Constitution granted all women the right to vote. But women didn't learn to use their power as voters until much later.

From the 1930s through the 1950s, women were more active in politics. But most did not run for office themselves. Instead they volunteered to work for other candidates — who were usually men.

In the 1960s, groups of women began working to help all women in their fight for equality. Women's roles in politics — in the U.S. and elsewhere — began to change. For example, a woman in Israel became head of state with her election as prime minister.

In the 1970s, two of the women in this book were elected to the U.S. Congress. A woman was named to the president's cabinet. And a woman was elected governor of Connecticut. But it all really began in 1917, with one Montana woman's election to the U.S. Congress.

ELLA GRASSO

. . . I realized early on that if I was concerned with problems, the best way of getting them solved was to be part of the decision-making process.

Ella Grasso

Following her election as the governor of Connecticut in 1974, Ella Grasso described herself as "the first lady governor who was not previously a governor's lady." She is one of a small number of women who have served as governors in the United States. The other women, however, have had one thing in common — each one's husband had been governor before her.

Ella was born in Windsor Locks, Connecticut, on May 10, 1919. Her parents came to the United

6

States from Italy. Ella Rosa Giovanna Oliva Tambussi, their only child, grew up in the same town where she was born.

Ella's hard work as a student earned her more than one scholarship which enabled her to continue her education. At Mount Holyoke College in Massachusetts she majored in economics and sociology.

Soon after receiving her master's degree in 1942, from Mount Holyoke College also, Ella married Tom Grasso. Tom was a schoolteacher whom Ella had known for most of her life.

Ella became involved in her first political adventure — the League of Women Voters — in 1943. "I am grateful to the league," she has explained, "because through the training I received there, I developed a real understanding of issues. And more than that, how to translate that into action. Positive action. I think that is why I went into government, because I realized early on that if I was concerned with problems, the best way of getting them solved was to be part of the decision-making process."

After working several years for the Democratic party — doing such things as writing campaign speeches and talking with voters on behalf of Democratic party candidates — Ella decided to run for office. Her first campaign was in 1952, when she was elected to the Connecticut legislature. She served two terms and, in 1958, was elected Connecticut's Secretary of State.

The secretary of state is a government official who is in charge of work done by the Department of State. One of the main functions of this department is maintaining official state records.

During twelve years in this state government position, Ella became one of the best known politicians in Connecticut. Throughout her political career, she has believed in asking the people what they want from their government. During her term as secretary of state, Ella turned her office in the state capitol building into a "people's lobby" where citizens from all over the state could visit to talk about government problems and seek advice.

In 1970, Ella was elected to the U.S. House of Representatives. Although she served two terms in Congress, she was not as successful at the national political level as she had been at the state level. Ella has said that she did not enjoy her time in Congress. She found congressional procedures "painfully slow," and she did not like living in Washington and having to be away from her family.

Ella returned to Connecticut and decided to run for governor. The leaders of the Democratic party in Connecticut didn't believe a woman could win. But Ella campaigned anyway.

At the start of her campaign, newspaper, radio and television reporters drew attention to the fact that she was a woman running for governor.

This disturbed Ella. She wanted it understood whether she was a woman or a man, people should vote for her because of her previous successes in state government. "The judgment will be made of me as an individual," she once said, "on the basis

Ella Grasso is pictured here on election night in
November 1974. When all the votes were in, she had been
elected governor of Connecticut.

9

of what I have accomplished in my career in public life and on the basis of what I'll be saying to the voters."

In the primary — an election in which candidates from the same party have been nominated, and one is elected as the choice of the party — she did well. Ella won the primary and became the Democratic candidate for governor.

During the 1974 campaign for governor, Ella's opponent Robert Steele began calling her "Spenderella" because of her campaign promises. If elected, Ella planned to spend money on new programs, but she promised not to raise taxes to pay for them. By naming her "Spenderella," Steele thought he was pointing out something that would cause her to lose the election. In fact, however, Ella's knowledge of another matter of "spending" money helped her win.

Ella conducted an investigation and let the people of Connecticut know the results. Former government officials had made a mistake and the people had been overcharged $19 million for utilities such as hot water, heat, and electricity.

In the final election, Ella beat her opponent Robert Steele by 200,000 votes. With her victory, she became one of the highest ranking women in United States politics.

After Ella was elected, she arranged for the state to borrow money for the utility companies, so they could pay for their operations without overcharging the people. But the state had other money problems, too.

When Ella was inaugurated as governor, she said, "Our state is in disarray." She warned the people of Connecticut to prepare themselves for hard times ahead as the government attempted to make up for a $70 million gap in the state budget.

As part of her program to cut back government spending, Ella started with herself. When she was given a $7,000 raise in her salary of $35,000, she turned the $7,000 back into the state treasury.

The steps she took to solve other problems, however, made her unpopular for a while. When the "hard times" arrived because of the cutback in government spending, some of the people complained. But time has passed since Ella took office as governor of Connecticut and things have improved.

Although Ella is the top government official in the state and her days are very busy, she still likes to talk personally with the people of Connecticut. These "talks" can occur in her office in the state capitol or as she's walking down the street — stopping along the way to exchange conversation. The days of the "people's lobby" have not ended.

Ella has shown time and again that her first concern is for the people of Connecticut. Her election record is proof of the success of her political career. In over a quarter of a century, Ella Grasso has not lost an election. From the Connecticut legislature in 1952, to the highest office in the state in 1974, she has continued to accept new challenges, and the people have continued to accept her.

LIZ HOLTZMAN

My victory says that no political figure, no matter how
powerful, can forget about the people he was elected to serve.
Liz Holtzman

If she won, she would be the youngest woman ever elected to Congress. If she won, it would be the first time her opponent had lost the election in fifty years. And if she won, her victory would be even more outstanding because she had very little money to conduct a campaign in her home district.

In an election which was called an "upset," Liz Holtzman did win. Experts who predict the outcomes of elections did not expect her to win. In

12

1972, at the age of thirty-one, Liz became the Democratic Congresswoman from Brooklyn, New York. She upset her opponent, Emanuel Celler, who had been in office for fifty years; and *Time* magazine dubbed her "Liz the Lion Killer."

Elizabeth Holtzman was born in Brooklyn, New York, on August 11, 1941. Her father, Sidney Holtzman, is a lawyer, and her mother, Filia Holtzman, is the chairperson of the Russian Department at Hunter College in New York. Liz has a twin brother, Robert, who is about one half-hour older than she is. He is a neurosurgeon.

Her first campaign for election came while she was in high school. She ran for vice-president of the student government, and her brother ran for president. They campaigned together, using the slogan "Win With the Twins," and they won.

Liz graduated *magna cum laude* ("with great distinction") from Radcliffe College in 1962. She enrolled at Harvard Law School that same year, and was one of fifteen women in a class of 500 men. She received her law degree in 1965 and went to work for a small law firm in New York.

Two years later she took a position as an assistant to John Lindsay, who was the mayor of New York City. As a mayoral assistant, Liz worked with the city department in charge of economic development, parks, recreation, and cultural affairs. Liz was successful in her job, but she was displeased because she saw many things in the government and political structure which she felt could be improved. She later told a newspaper reporter,

"The agencies just weren't responding to the public needs."

Believing that human needs should come first, Liz Holtzman decided to run for public office and try to do something about it. In 1970, she was elected a Democratic State Committeewoman. In this position, which she filled for two years, she worked within the Democratic party to make it stronger.

In 1972, the famous campaign of "Liz the Lion Killer" took place. Liz beat opponent Emanuel Celler in the primary — an election in which candidates from the same party have been nominated, and the one who receives the most votes is elected as the choice of the party. Both Liz and Emanuel Celler were Democratic party candidates. When Liz beat Celler, she knew that she would probably win the general election later in the year.

Because she had little money to spend, Liz's campaign was conducted mainly on foot. She rang doorbells and shook hands in subways, supermarkets, shopping centers, laundromats, and at bus stops. After her election, Liz said kiddingly that she owed her success to the movie *The Godfather*. During her campaign she would stand outside the Brooklyn theatres where the movie was being shown and talk with the thousands of people who lined up to see it.

In the November 1972 election, Liz beat her Republican opponent, Nicholas R. Macchio. She received 96,984 votes to his 33,828. Following her

Liz Holtzman (right) and her mother are shown at the campaign headquarters of Ms. Holtzman. Liz went on to be elected to Congress from the state of New York.

victory, the new member of the U.S. House of Representatives said to her supporters, "We made a point in this campaign. The political pros tend to underestimate the people and we proved them wrong. The people are very concerned about having youthful, vigorous representation . . ."

Though Liz Holtzman's victory was one of the biggest political upsets of 1972, most people know of her for work she has done since she was elected. As a member of the House Judiciary Committee, Liz won national fame during the committee's 1974 hearings on the impeachment of former President Richard Nixon. The Judiciary Committee decides whether people are being treated fairly and whether the government is following the law outlined in the Constitution.

15

Liz Holtzman discusses strategy with a Judiciary Committee lawyer during the impeachment hearings of President Richard M. Nixon in 1974.

Liz Holtzman's contributions to the House of Representatives and the American people have not been limited to her work with the Judiciary Committee. She has been supportive of legislation that would provide government money for local law enforcement, housing for poor people, and food stamps for people who receive Social Security benefits.

Because of her support of legislation to help women, Liz has been called "the leader of the Women's Movement in the House." She earned

16

this title because of her work for better abortion laws, programs to help women when they retire and laws to make it illegal to fire a woman because of pregnancy.

Congresswoman Holtzman travels from Washington, D.C., to her office in Brooklyn twice a week to talk with the people in her district. The voters tell her what they need and want from their government, and Liz works hard to get it. But there are still some people who are against women being involved in politics and elected to government offices.

These people say women "aren't strong enough." Liz Holtzman thinks just the opposite is true. "There is widespread alienation," she has said, "against government — it takes taxes and ignores needs. I think people feel they can trust a woman because she won't get involved in backroom cigar-smoking politics."

Elizabeth Holtzman has apparently earned the trust of the people from the Brooklyn, New York, district she represents. In 1978, she was elected to her fourth term in the U.S. House of Representatives. Her first campaign for Congress was in 1972. Recalling that time she has said, "I found mothers taking their daughters up to meet me. They wanted their daughters to have a different conception of the possibilities for them."

The possibilities for young women entering politics — and the possibilities for Congresswoman Holtzman to continue to have new successes in her political career — seem unlimited.

BARBARA JORDAN

The long-range hope I have for this country is that it will grow stronger and that everybody can feel that they're in it, that it really does belong to us.

Barbara Jordan

Barbara Jordan is a black woman. She's from Texas and has been an elected member of the United States House of Representatives. Because she is black and because she is a woman, she had to overcome obstacles which most politicians have never had to face.

As a past member of Congress, Barbara's main interest was in a document that's almost 200 years old — the Constitution of the United States. Her goal was to make sure that people had the equal rights which the Constitution promises them.

"'We, the people.'" Barbara quoted the beginning of the Constitution, "— it is a very eloquent beginning. But when the Constitution of the United States was completed on the 17th of September in 1787, I was not included in that 'We, the people.' I felt for many years that somehow George Washington and Alexander Hamilton just left me out by mistake. But through the process of amendment, interpretation, and court decision, I have finally been included in 'We, the people . . .'"

She feels she has now been included because parts of the Constitution have been changed. The laws of this country are based on what is written in the Constitution, changes — or amendments — can be made to it if the people vote for them. The Nineteenth Amendment is an example of a change to the Constitution which gave women the right to vote.

By the word "interpretation," Barbara was talking about the meaning or explanation which people today give for parts of the Constitution — some things written such a long time ago can have different meanings today. "Court decision" refers to the fact that some courts of law can decide whether something is in agreement or disagreement with the Constitution, and therefore with the laws of this country.

Barbara Jordan was born on February 21, 1936, in Houston, Texas. She is the youngest of Arlyne and Benjamin Jordan's three daughters. "We were poor," Barbara has said, "but so was everyone around us so we didn't notice it. We were never hungry and we always had a place to stay."

Benjamin Jordan, a Baptist minister who also worked as a warehouse clerk, had high expectations of his children. Barbara, however, set equally high standards for herself. "She was unhappy," her father said, "if she made less than a straight A average in school."

As a high school student, Barbara decided she wanted to be something outstanding when she grew up. "I never wanted to be run-of-the-mill," she has said: "I always wanted to be something unusual." But she didn't know what until she heard a speech by Edith Sampson during a Career Day assembly at high school. Edith Sampson was a lawyer. And, that's what Barbara decided she wanted to be.

Barbara enrolled at Texas Southern University, a college for black students, in 1952. Besides studying, she participated in many school activities. She was elected to the student council, worked as editor of the yearbook, and was a champion member of the debating team. She graduated *magna cum laude* ("with great distinction"), with a degree in political science and history, in 1956.

Her next goal was to be accepted to a law school. In 1956, Harvard Law School was considered the "best," and that's where Barbara wanted to go. But Harvard did not accept her. Instead, she became the first woman and the first black person to enter Boston University Law School. Three years later she graduated.

In 1960, law degree in hand, Barbara returned to Texas and set up her law practice — on her parent's dining room table. She didn't have enough money to open an office of her own. During this time, she also began campaigning for the Democratic nominee for president, John F. Kennedy, and his running mate, Lyndon B. Johnson. And, she worked on a few campaigns of her own. In 1962, and again in 1964, Barbara ran for the Texas State Legislature, but she wasn't elected.

A new voting district was formed in Texas in 1966. The people in this district were mainly black and Mexican-American, and they elected Barbara Jordan to the state legislature. Although she was the first black woman ever elected to the Texas State Senate, Barbara did not use her race or sex as a campaign issue. Other people did, however, both to help her and hurt her. But Barbara's campaign promises had included plans to help better the lives of all Texans, not just black people or women.

Barbara served two successful terms in the state legislature. About one-half of the bills she submitted to the state governing body were made into laws. She fought for better laws for the "really poor people, laundry workers, domestics, [and] farm workers."

President Lyndon B. Johnson, a Texan like Barbara, noticed that she was concerned about laws which were unfair to the "common" people. Barbara and President Johnson were both working for passage of civil rights laws. Civil rights are personal liberties guaranteed to all. President Johnson said of Barbara, "She proved that black is beautiful before we knew what it meant . . . She is involved in a government system of all the people, all the races, all economic groups." President Johnson was supportive of Barbara's political endeavors until his death in 1973.

In 1972, Barbara was elected to the U.S. House of Representatives. She was the second black woman ever elected to Congress — Shirley Chisholm was the first. After her election, she wanted to be appointed to the House Judiciary Commitee.

The Judiciary Committee decides whether people are being treated fairly and whether the government is following the law outlined in the Constitution. Barbara knew the Judiciary Committee would probably review issues related to civil rights legislation. Civil rights issues were important to the people in the Texas district she represented. And, because of her law background, she knew she could be useful on the committee.

She was assigned to the Judiciary Committee, and, in 1974, became nationally famous for her involvement in the impeachment hearings concerning former President Nixon. The hearings were to decide whether Nixon had committed illegal acts as president. During this time, Barbara said, "My faith in the Constitution is whole, it is complete, it is total. I am not going to sit here and be an idle spectator to the . . . destruction of the Constitution."

Two years after the impeachment hearings, Bar-

Barbara Jordan is shown at graduation exercises at the University of Cincinnati in 1976. She had recently been named as a possible vice presidential candidate.

bara achieved another "first." In 1976, she served as the keynote speaker at the Democratic National Convention. This was the first time a black or a woman was the main speaker at a national party convention. During her speech on this occasion,

23

she was interrupted twenty-four times by people clapping for her.

In her speech, she talked about her favorite topic — equality for all people. She said no people should be treated specially just because they are rich or powerful. She said rich and powerful people should follow the rules just like poor people. Barbara also said all people should share the responsibility for making the country better.

She is an example of a person who has shared the responsibility for improving conditions in the United States. As a Congresswoman, Barbara was proudest of what she did to give blacks and Spanish-speaking people a chance for better lives.

There are about one-half million people in the Texas district she represented. Almost half of these people are black, and another large number of them are Mexican-American. Almost all of them are poor. Barbara worked for laws to stop discrimination and to help people receive fair treatment from businesses and other institutions.

This woman who has accomplished so much in her political career did not seek reelection in 1978. "I'm at a juncture where I want to regain control of my life," she said. She explained that she needed more time for herself and for her own life. Many people did not want her to quit politics, but she felt the need to find other ways to express her views and work for the things she believes in.

Even as a young student, Barbara was never interested in "popularity contests." And, as a politician who campaigned to be elected, she still

Barbara Jordan stands before the Democratic convention in 1976. She is about to give the keynote speech.

wasn't interested in just being popular. Her main interest as an elected official was to work for each person in the United States to have an equal chance to succeed and lead a happy life.

Barbara firmly believes the United States belongs to the people. She once said, "The long-range hope I have for this country is that it will grow stronger and that everybody can feel that they're in it, that it really does belong to us . . . . I want to see the day when we — everybody — can feel like we belong here, that this country has to survive because we have to survive, that our future is bound up in the future of the nation."

Whatever Barbara's future decisions are, her contributions to the American people have not been small. And, her life has been far from "run-of-the-mill."

JUANITA KREPS

I was always interested in social problems . . . If you read the newspapers and had a sense of where the world was, you couldn't help being concerned. I thought economics would give me more insight into what was going on.

Juanita M. Kreps

Juanita M. Kreps talks with President Jimmy Carter on a regular basis, and he listens attentively. As a matter of fact, she is one of a small group of people who are paid to tell the President of the United States what to do. Juanita talks to President Carter about economics — the financial situation in the United States.

One of the first things a new president does is select a Cabinet. The Cabinet is made up of people who advise the president on different government issues. Each member of this group is in charge of a different aspect of government. The Cabinet member is considered an expert in his or her area of responsibility. These people make important decisions to help the government operate smoothly.

When Jimmy Carter chose his Cabinet in 1977, women all over the country wanted him to select women for some of these important jobs. But women haven't been active in politics for a very long time, and Jimmy Carter said there weren't many "qualified" women to choose from. He was criticized for this comment, and he did choose two women.

One of the women was Juanita M. Kreps of North Carolina. She was named Secretary of the Commerce Department — the first woman to ever be appointed to that position and the fourth woman in American history to be named to a Cabinet post.

Juanita knows more than most people about economics. In fact, she has devoted her career to it. In college, she recalls, "I was always interested in social problems . . . If you read the newspapers and had a sense of where the world was, you couldn't help being concerned. I thought economics would give me more insight into what was going on." Now she is part of what is going on.

At the age of fifty-eight, Juanita can look back on a life that has not been without excitement or challenges. Her father was a struggling coal mine operator in Kentucky. Juanita, the sixth child of

Juanita Kreps is shown with President Carter in 1976.
She had just been named Secretary of Commerce.

Elmer and Larcenia Morris, was born on January 11, 1921 in Lynch, Kentucky.

She attended Berea College in her home state. Berea was a small college that offered a special program to help poor students work their way through school. Juanita believes the school helped shape her life. "The spirit of the place," she has said, "was one of independence, self-reliance, high-level integrity and academic excellence. It made a deeper impression on me than did my childhood."

After graduating from Berea in 1942, Juanita attended Duke University where she received her Master's Degree and doctorate in economics. She excelled in school and was admitted to the Phi Beta Kappa national honor society. After college, Juanita married Dr. Clifton Kreps, Jr., who is a professor of banking at the University of North Carolina. The Kreps family includes Juanita, Clifton, and their three grown children.

As an economist and an advisor to the president, Juanita studies businesses, corporations, and foreign governments; and she studies the products and services these organizations offer to people in the United States. Part of her job is to know what products and services people want from companies and businesses. She investigates programs the government offers people — such as educational programs and health care programs. As an economist, she needs to know how much money these products and programs cost, how much the people are willing to spend, and how much the government can get in return.

As the Secretary of the Commerce Department, Juanita Kreps is officially in charge of seeing that her department will "encourage, serve and promote the nation's economic development and technological advancement." This means her responsibility is to help the country produce more and better things so that more money is received for what is made and sold.

Juanita, however, believes the major role of the Commerce Department is to "encourage business to perform well all tasks that improve human welfare." A big part of business and economics is the people involved — the workers and the customers. Juanita likes the "human" side of business. She wants to improve the lives of workers and of consumers — the people who buy the products made by workers.

The Commerce Department handles many different problems and kinds of work in its efforts to improve the economic system in the United States. About 38,000 employees in the department work in areas which range from forecasting the weather to testing products before they are sold to people.

Juanita has worked especially hard to help women and older working people. She feels that businesses will have to make changes in the future to fit the changes happening in the world.

She thinks businesses can help solve those problems and she is working to help them do just that. By visiting different business people in their own areas, Juanita also tries to understand their needs and problems so that she can help solve them.

Juanita Kreps does not consider herself a women's liberationist. But she has been in the forefront of the fight for equality of opportunity for women.

And, in 1977, when President Carter made the comment that it was difficult to find qualified women in his search for each Cabinet post, Juanita said, "We simply have to do a better job of looking." She explained that she thought it would be difficult to defend the notion "that there are not a great many qualified women."

In all this woman has done — her work with Congress, her meetings with business people all over the nation, and her regular sessions with President Carter — she has frequently been described as "firm" and "charming."

Having worked with Juanita, one government official was quoted as saying, "I've never known (of) anyone walking away mad after an argument with Juanita, but she's tough — she makes her point of view known."

It seems that many people are interested in her "point of view." Juanita M. Kreps who once said, "I was always interested in social problems," has the talent and energy to do something about them.

GOLDA MEIR

No people is an island. We are bound to each other by the problems of our region, our world. We can make of these ties a curse or a blessing. Each nation, each land must decide.
                                                      Golda Meir

More than thirty years ago, a hopeful and fearful Golda Meir came to the United States on a very important mission. She had volunteered to raise a huge sum of money which would determine whether the nation of Israel could continue its struggle for independence.

Plain in appearance, a middle-aged woman with graying hair tied back in a bun — Golda had just arrived and was about to make her first speech. She was scared, but she was determined.

Some of the richest and most powerful people in America sat waiting before her. In the next few minutes she would ask this important collection of people for money — millions of dollars.

She spoke and the audience listened attentively. When she finished, they stood and cheered. Her request that the American Jewish people aid the people of Israel in their fight for a Jewish homeland was answered with pledges of money that totaled $25 million.

From donations by both Jewish and non-Jewish people, Golda Meir raised a total of $50 million.

Goldie Mabovitch, who would later be known as Golda Meir, was born in Kiev, Russia, on May 3, 1898. When she was eight years old, Golda and her family moved to the United States.

Even as a young girl, Golda was interested in a group of people's belief that a free national Jewish community could be set up near the Mediterranean Sea in Palestine, part of which is known today as Israel. For centuries, Jewish people were often ruled by leaders of countries where Jews were not wanted. This group of people who wanted to establish a nation for Jews were called Zionists.

During her high school years, Golda's belief in the Zionist movement continued to grow. After graduating from teacher's college, Golda taught in a school in Milwaukee where the other teachers, including herself, were Zionists.

When she was nineteen, Golda married Morris Meyerson. She continued her political work, traveling around the country making speeches and raising money for the Labor Zionist Party.

Four years later, in 1921, Golda and Morris, and several other Zionists, sailed to Palestine. Soon after their arrival, Golda and Morris moved into the Merhavia Kibbutz. A kibbutz is a farm or settlement where everyone shares the responsibilities and the land. Women and men are equal in the kibbutz, and everyone works together for the common goals of the settlement.

Morris, however, was not suited for kibbutz life — either physically or mentally. When he became ill, they left the kibbutz and moved to Tel Aviv in 1923. A year later, they moved to Jerusalem. Morris worked as a bookkeeper and Golda took in laundry to earn money. They had two children, born in 1924 and 1926.

During the next twenty years, Golda worked in many different Jewish organizations. She was most active in the Histradrut Council — also called the General Federation of Jewish Labor. This organization's purpose was to uphold the rights of workers in Palestine. And, because of a new position with the Histradrut, in 1945, it was necessary for Golda to move to Tel Aviv.

On November 29, 1947, the United Nations voted to divide Palestine into two parts — an Arab state and a Jewish state. But Arab nations were against dividing Palestine, and they threatened war — if Israel declared its independence.

Three days after the United Nations proposed dividing Palestine, groups of Arabs began rioting. Israel did not have the military power or the money to buy the weapons necessary to fight the Arabs for their independence. So Golda traveled to the United States where she raised $50 million for her people.

On Friday, May 14, 1948, the Jewish state became a reality for 650,000 people who lived there. The nation called Israel would be a place for Jewish people to live in freedom.

The following morning, war began. The new state of Israel was attacked by countries on all sides.

After a short time, David Ben-Gurion — the first Prime Minister of Israel — asked Golda to be Israel's Minister of Labor. It was the kind of job Golda wanted — she could live in Israel and work to help the people of her country.

In January 1949, Golda was elected to the first Knesset (Israeli legislature). The Arab nations and Israel had been at war since May 1948. The fighting "officially" ended in the spring of 1949 when the warring nations signed peace agreements. But the problems were not solved.

Golda took office as the Minister of Labor in April 1949. Her responsibility was to provide work and housing for the nearly 1,000 new imigrants who arrived in Israel daily. By the end of 1951, nearly 700,000 Jews arrived in Israel to live. She described her seven years as Minister of Labor as "the most satisfying and the happiest" of her life.

In 1956, Ben-Gurion asked Golda to become the Foreign Minister. He also ordered her to change

This picture shows Golda Meir in a thoughtful mood. It was taken in 1960 in Milwaukee, Wisconsin.

her last name from Meyerson to a Hebrew name. She chose Meir, which means "illuminate."

Golda entered the Foreign Ministry in the summer of 1956. A major part of her job was meeting with leaders of other countries to try to find solutions to the problems between Israel and the Arab states.

But her most important contribution as Foreign Minister was that she organized programs to help other developing nations. As part of this effort, Israeli experts in agriculture, engineering, medicine and other fields shared their knowledge with people from other developing countries.

Golda continued as Foreign Minister for nearly ten years. During this time, her good friend Levi Eshkol replaced Ben-Gurion as Prime Minister. In 1965, Golda retired from public office. She told Eshkol, "I do want to be able to read a book without feeling guilty . . . and I don't want to see another airport for several years."

But retirement did not last long. After a few months, Golda was asked to return to politics. She agreed to serve as secretary-general of the Labor Zionist Party because her help was needed. In the meantime, the Arabs began preparing once again for war. This time the war lasted only six days, and Israel won. But it was not the last war the young country would face.

On February 26, 1969, Prime Minister Eshkol died, and the Labor Party asked Golda to become the Prime Minister. It was difficult, at seventy, for her to decide to accept this responsibility. But she

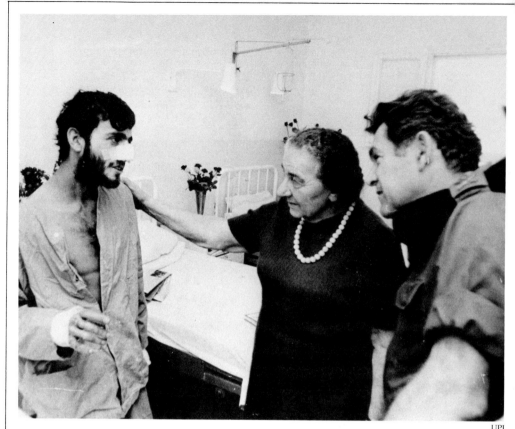

Golda Meir and an Israeli general (right) talk with a
soldier who had been wounded in the Yom Kippur War.

did. And she soon faced one of the biggest
problems of her career — the Yom Kippur War.

Yom Kippur is a Jewish religious holiday, "the
most solemn and sacred of all the days in the
Jewish calendar," as Golda described it. On this
day, October 6, 1973, a forceful attack by Arab
troops took Israel by surprise, and a full-scale war
followed.

The day before the Yom Kippur holiday, Golda
had been concerned that something was about to
happen. But her cabinet advised her not to call the
Israeli military forces into action. When Golda's

fears were realized, Israeli forces quickly prepared, and, in the end, won the war. But many lives had been lost the first few days of the fighting, and people blamed Golda and her advisors for being unprepared.

Though the war had ended, clashes continued over which land would belong to which country. And, there were other conflicts — within the Israeli government — about how the war was handled and how the country should be run. On April 10, 1975, at the age of seventy-five, Golda retired for the last time. She told the Knesset "Five years are sufficient. It is beyond my strength to continue carrying this burden . . ."

On June 4, Golda Meir left office. She died three years later. In her autobiography, written in 1975, that plain-looking, determined woman gave thanks for the life she lived.

"My life has been greatly blessed. Not only have I lived to see the State of Israel born, but I have also seen it take in and successfully absorb masses of Jews from all parts of the world . . . it is I who am indebted for what has been given me from the time I first learned about Zionism . . . all the way through to my half century here, where I have seen my five grandchildren grow up as free Jews in a country that is their own."

JEANNETTE RANKIN

I want to stand by my country, but I cannot vote for war.
Jeannette Rankin

A group of 389 people are deciding whether the United States will declare war on another country. When the time comes for each to vote by saying yea or nay, only one says, "Nay." She continues, "As a woman I can't go to war, and I refuse to send anyone else." The vote was 388 to 1, and the United States entered World War II in 1941. The group of voters were members of the United States Congress.

Jeannette Rankin, sixty years old at the time, was the only person to vote against the United

States declaring war on Japan. This was the second time she'd been outvoted on the subject of war. The first time was in 1917, when she and forty-eight other members of Congress voted against declaring war on Germany and entering World War I.

At the age of eighty-seven, in 1968, Jeannette Rankin was still firm in her belief that disagreements could be settled in a peaceful manner. At this time, she led a group of 5,000 women who called themselves the "Jeannette Rankin Brigade" in a peaceful demonstration in Washington, D.C., to show the President and other government officials that they did not believe the United States should be fighting the war in Vietnam.

Jeannette Rankin was a pacifist. A pacifist is a person who does not believe in war. When two or more countries or groups of people disagree about something, they sometimes declare war on each other to settle the argument. Pacifists do not believe in war, killing, or violence for any reason. Jeannette Rankin dedicated her life to pacifist causes and equal rights for women.

Jeannette was born on June 11, 1880, in Montana — nine years before Montana became a state. Jeannette's father, whom she was very close to, was a farmer. As she grew up, Jeannette was not sure what she wanted to do in her lifetime.

She lived at home while she attended the University of Montana in Missoula. After she graduated from college in 1902, she was qualified to teach school. But Jeannette was anxious for something else to happen in her life. In this same year, she wrote in her diary, "Go! Go! Go! It makes no difference where, just so you go! go! go! Remember, at the first opportunity, go!"

She tried teaching, dressmaking, and furniture designing, but none of these satisfied her need for something that was both exciting and worthwhile. Finally, in 1904, Jeannette traveled to Boston. In Boston, she had her first look at real poverty. She was shocked by the big-city slums and the terrible living conditions.

Four years later, Jeannette moved to San Francisco where she began her career as a social worker. After a short time, she decided that to be most useful, she needed to learn more about her new occupation. So she moved to New York City and enrolled in a school which later became the Columbia University School for Social Work. As a student there, Jeannette's awareness of social injustice increased, and her concern for underpriviliged people continued to grow.

In 1910, she accepted a job in a children's home in Spokane, Washington. After a few weeks, she decided that she would not be able to change the "appalling" conditions that she found existed in the home. She quit the job and enrolled at the University of Washington in Seattle. She studied economics, sociology, and public speaking. This was the beginning of her interest in politics, and a way that she could help people.

She began working, that same year, for passage of the Nineteenth Amendment, which would give women the right to vote. For the next five years, Jeannette devoted her time and energy to campaigning in Washington, California, Montana and other states for the cause of women's suffrage — the right of voting. The Nineteenth Amendment would not be passed as a constitutional amendment — thus giving women in all states the right to vote — until 1920. Many states, however, gave women voting privileges before suffrage was granted nationally.

Montana granted women the right to vote in 1914. And, in 1916, Jeannette decided to run for the U.S. Congress, as Montana's delegate to the House of Representatives.

Most people predicted that Jeannette would lose the election. But she won and, in 1916, became the first woman ever elected to Congress. She was thirty-six years old at the time.

About winning this first major election, Jeannette said many years later, "We got the vote in Montana because the spirit of the pioneer days was still alive. Men thought of women in the same terms they thought of themselves." When pioneers settled in the West in the early 1900s, men and women worked alongside each other, sharing the danger and work, and solving the problems of settling a new frontier. For this reason, many of the Western and Midwestern states gave women the right to vote before the Eastern states.

During her two-year term in Congress, 1917-1919, Jeannette's greatest contribution was furthering of the cause of women's suffrage. She also introduced the first bill that would have allowed women citizenship independent of their husbands. She proposed a maternity and infant health bill that became law in 1921. And, finally, she proposed and committed herself to peace.

In 1917, she voted against the United States declaring war on Germany. Although forty-eight other people voted the same way, newspaper reporters singled Jeannette out of the group for criticism. They wrote that she was cowardly and not loyal to her country.

Speaking of the incident many years later, she said, "I felt at the time that the first woman (in Congress) should take the first stand, that the first time the first woman had a chance to say no to war she should say it."

Although Jeannette wanted to run for a second term in the U.S. House of Representatives, she didn't. Montana had been divided into two voting districts, rather than one, and Jeannette wanted to represent all the people of the state — not just those in one district. So, she decided to run for the U.S. Senate instead.

She felt that her performance in Congress had proved her a good representative of the people. But there were two major things against her in this bid for a different political office. First, it was unlikely that a woman would be elected to the Senate. Second, her vote against the United States entering World War I had made her seem weak to many voters. She lost the Senate election — but

Jeannette Rankin is shown testifying before a congressional committee in 1939. She was speaking against making the U.S. Navy larger.

only by 1,714 votes.

When Jeannette's congressional term in the House ended in 1919, she stayed in Washington, D.C., and continued to fight for better working conditions for women and children and for other social causes. Although Jeannette was dedicated to social welfare and was successful with reform in that area, the peace movement was the cause she eventually dedicated herself to completely.

In the 1930s, Jeannette was active in a group called the National Council for Prevention of War. As a member of this peace group, she tried to persuade congressional members to use their power to do things to prevent war.

In 1940, nearly twenty years after her first term in office, Jeannette announced her intention to, once again, run for Congress as a representative from her home state Montana. She was sixty years old at the time, and she won election to the U.S. House of Representatives. Ironically, one of the first major congressional votes she participated in concerned war — whether the United States would declare war on Japan.

This time, however, she was the only person to vote against war. People begged her to change her vote. But Jeannette's belief in peace was the philosophy of her life. To vote for war would have been to vote against her life. She was strong in her opinion on the subject and later explained to a friend, "What one decides to do in a crisis depends on one's philosophy of life, and that

Jeannette Rankin (fourth from the right) helps hold a sign during a women's anti-war protest in Washington, D. C., in 1968.

philosophy cannot be changed by an incident . . ."

Jeannette Rankin died three weeks before her ninety-third birthday in 1973. As a young woman, she worked for women's suffrage. In later years, she was active in the women's rights movement.

But the cause that remained closest to Jeannette's heart was her unyielding belief in peace. Equally strong was her belief that women could be successful in achieving this goal. She felt that women should be more involved in politics.

"The men have taught women not to trust their emotions," she said, "but women have an emotional ideal to contribute, and if they organized we could have peace in one year."

BIBLIOGRAPHY

Agress, Eliyahu. *Golda Meir: Portrait of a Prime Minister.* New York: Sabra Books, [1969].

Chamberlin, Hope. *Minority of Members: Women in the U.S. Congress.* New York: New American Library, 1974.

Christopher, Maurine. *Black Americans in Congress.* rev. ed. Scranton, Penn.: Thomas Y. Crowell, 1976.

Haskins, James. *Barbara Jordan.* New York: Dial Press 1977.

Josephson, Hannah. *Jeannette Rankin: First Lady in Congress.* Indianapolis, Ind.: Bobbs-Merrill, 1974.

McDowell, Barbara, ed., and Umlauf, Hana, ed. *The Good Housekeeping Woman's Almanac.* New York: Newspaper Enterprise Association, 1977.

Mann, Peggy. *Golda: The Story of Israel's Prime Minister.* East Rutherford, N.J.: Coward, McCann & Geoghegan, 1971.

Meir, Golda. *My Life.* New York: G.P. Putnam's Sons, 1975.

Tolchin, Susan, and Tolchin, Martin. *Clout: Womanpower and Politics.* East Rutherford, N.J.: G.P. Putnam's Sons, 1974 .